12# From Brokenness
To Blooming

Poems to Soothe and Heal the Soul

Zia Marshall

notionpress.com

INDIA · SINGAPORE · MALAYSIA

Copyright © Zia Marshall 2023
All Rights Reserved.

ISBN 979-8-89133-756-5

This book has been published with all efforts taken to make the material error-free after the consent of the author. However, the author and the publisher do not assume and hereby disclaim any liability to any party for any loss, damage, or disruption caused by errors or omissions, whether such errors or omissions result from negligence, accident, or any other cause.

While every effort has been made to avoid any mistake or omission, this publication is being sold on the condition and understanding that neither the author nor the publishers or printers would be liable in any manner to any person by reason of any mistake or omission in this publication or for any action taken or omitted to be taken or advice rendered or accepted on the basis of this work. For any defect in printing or binding the publishers will be liable only to replace the defective copy by another copy of this work then available.

"A poem…begins as a lump in the throat, a sense of wrong, a homesickness…. It is a reaching-out toward expression; an effort to find fulfillment. A complete poem is one where an emotion finds the thought and the thought finds the words."

— Robert Frost

I dedicate this book to all those who have suffered from trauma so that I may offer an understanding of the nature of suffering and the many complicated shades of grieving and healing from loss.

Author's Note

This book is for those who have waded through the lonely sea of trauma. The poems in this collection will help you rise from chaos to find the strength to navigate the rough waters and eventually reach the shores of healing. If your trauma has made you feel like a ship cast adrift in a violent storm, the poems in this collection will offer the shelter of a safe harbor. This book will help you move from pieces to eventual peace as you turn away from the darkness of being broken apart and move towards the light of gratitude and joy.

In short, this book offers a safe space for you to dwell on your trauma, when no other place fits. You can both grieve here, my friend, and find the solace and the strength to heal.

Contents

1. The Shattering 9
2. The Rising 31
3. The Strengthening 41
4. The Healing. 59
5. The Ruminating 85
6. The Growing 119
7. The Rejoicing 133
8. The Blooming 143

The Shattering

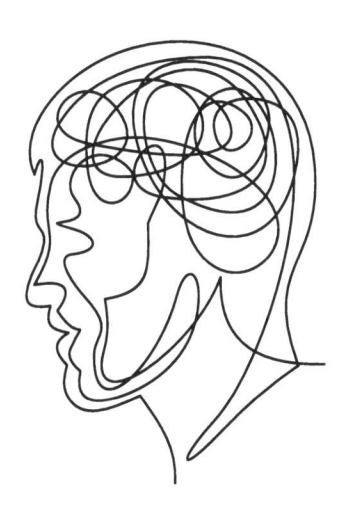

Fire Child

Sweet One! Today you feel
battered and bruised.
Maybe even a little broken,
a little worn around the edges.

But I promise, one day,
you will look back at this time
and see it for what it really was.
And that is when it will dawn on you!

There is so much to learn from
all the aching and the breaking
and the falling and the shattering.
And when you hit rock bottom,

you'll realize it wasn't the undoing of you.
It was the making of you
into who you are today.
A Fire child!

For aren't you flying now, Sweet One?

Betrayal

Walking down the pathway of life,
she navigated the slippery slope of stress and strife.
It was all part of the bargain she called life.
She learned to take it in her stride.

Till one cold February Monday,
when winter's last chill lingered in the air.
She tasted the bitter drink called betrayal.
Her heart hung heavy, her grief a tangible thing in the air.

She tried to ignore betrayal's bitter truth.
Coils of friendship turned into venomous snakes.
The twisted lies, the deceit, the unending hurt,
and through it all she forgave and forgave for love's sake.

She refused to lash out; refused to fight.
Didn't an eye for an eye turn the world blind?
But when friendship stripped off its mask revealed its harsh light.
Emptiness is all you find, all you find.

In a world made of steel, made of stone,
she cried bitter tears; wiped them dry.
Squaring her shoulders, she learned to walk alone
to a silent place of peace and solitude.

Letting Go

She asked for kindness and compassion.
She didn't find that in abundance.
She asked for laughter and simplicity.
She received untruth and inauthenticity.
After a barrage of bitter innuendoes,
she could wrestle no more.
So, she let it go...let it go.

And if it made her cry
to bid goodbye,
she would make her tired soul understand.
For the first rule of any relationship
be it kinship or friendship
is to be plainspoken, honest and steadfast...like a lighthouse aglow,
a beacon of strength to those who approach.

Incredibly Broken, Incredibly Beautiful

Despite all the ways the world has broken her, every morning, she tucks courage in her soul and hope in her heart and shows up in a million ways. And I think that is incredibly beautiful.

Your Soul Sister

Life has fallen apart for you again and again. More times than you can count. And each time, you lose touch with her. Your sacred inner self. Your soul sister who dwells within you. The self full of meaning and brimful of life. The self who is not afraid to be unapologetically herself. The girl with sunflowers in her eyes and fire in her heart. The girl who skips through life. So Sweet One, it is time to stop crawling in the shadows and take your place in the sun. You belong here.

Who Loves Me Enough?

Who loves me enough to see through my smiles
at the pain hidden in these broken eyes?
Who loves me enough to let me to take down my smile;
show the quiet despair hidden deep inside?

My breaking, my pain has taught me softness,
kindness in the face of merciless ugliness.
For one who has borne pain can never inflict it on another.
She carries love in her heart to care and nurture.

But who loves me enough to care for me when I am worn?
Enough to say "lean on me, I'll hold you through the storm."
So instead of pushing and straining my muscle and sinew,
I might just let the tension fade, rejuvenate.

Who loves me enough to listen to my ugly?
The despair, the pain, the sadness, the barbarity!
Who loves me enough not to be scared away,
by an uncertainty that sings night and day, night and day?

Who loves me enough, so I don't need to be strong,
when I am messy, fragmented, weak, all wrong?
Who loves me enough through my happy-sad duality?
The sunshine and shadows that dance through my disparity.

Who loves me enough not to spurn me on difficult days?
The days when my scars surface and stay.
And who loves me enough when I triumph through it all?
When I stumble, fall. Bear it all, stand tall!

Who loves me for the inner me?
Not all the roles I play, now a Lion, now a Sheep!
Who loves me enough to soothe my tired brow when I sleep?
Let my tears roll; just let me weep.

And who loves me enough to fight the world for me?
Talk of my strength, my inner light, when people hurl nasty.
And who loves me enough to fend off the blows,
so that I can rest my head on my soft pillow.

Dueling with Damage

At first it will break you,
not into tidy little pieces,
which can easily be put back together.
The breaking is
messy and ugly.

You will shatter
into a million pieces
and for all the world
you will feel like you will never be whole again.
It hurts like hell. But this is

not the hard part.
The hard part
is the healing
when you struggle to emerge
from the fragments of your damage.

Slowly you learn to embrace
your scars and blemishes.
And you learn how easy it is
to lose the kindness and compassion
that lie at the core of your being.

And you struggle very, very hard
to hold on to your kindness.

Trauma

Don't swallow your trauma.
Give voice to it.
Speak it aloud for all to hear.

And if people shuffle their feet in discomfort,
still remain unequivocally loud about your trauma.

Own your trauma,
but don't own any shame attached to it.

The trauma, and the sorrow, and the healing belong to you.
Own them but never bow your head because of them.

The Colors of Trauma

Trauma's first color is red.
The red of rage that storms through the world on wings of fire,
shattering everything in its wake.

Trauma's second color is grey.
The grey of grief that hangs in the air like heavy mist
and envelops your heart, mind and soul.

Trauma's third color is gold.
The gold of healing.
And all the cracks in broken souls
are filled with the liquid sparkle of gold
so that they are once again made whole.
Gold that acts as a soothing balm for broken spirits
and makes them worthy and strong once more.

Trauma last color is rainbow.
All the colors meld and blend
into a rainbow of powerful emotions.
You will never forget what you have gone through,
but you will use the rainbow
to remind you of all the hues of life
that went into the making of you.

Falling Apart

Some people break apart and go silent.
Some people break apart and talk about it.
Some people break apart and create something beautiful from their pain.

Everyone has their own way of surviving trauma.
And there is no right or wrong way either.

Making a Home of Trauma

The thing is even trauma starts to
feel like home at times.
And if you allow it to, it will settle into
the very marrow of your bones.

Bitter, corrosive brokenness
can creep all over you like ivy
and just stay there looking pretty.

So you have to tear out your weeds
with your own hands
even if they bleed.
And then spit them out of your garden hearts.

Tryst with Trauma

When the tsunami of trauma enters your life,
it swallows you whole.
And your grief becomes a fortress.
Your shattered being your cage
in which you shut yourself away from the world.

And the only way out of the cage is in.
The inward journey you need to make
to walk away from the shadows
and find your place in the sun.
And when brief moments of joy

flash across your soul,
you learn to once more open
the floodgates of your heart
and let in laughter
and sunshine and mirth.

And slowly you learn to breathe!
Not gulp in air
like a person starved for oxygen,
but breathe gently as you release the hurt.
And while you may never be able

to control the storms in the skies
that darken your journey through life,
you can rest safe in the knowledge that
you will learn to glide through life
cutting a wide swathe through the trauma waters.

No one encounters trauma and comes out unscathed.
But all of us choose different paths to healing
and all of us emerge different individuals.
I have yet to meet a person unaltered by damage.

Shades of Grief

When I am caught in a great sorrow storm
and I can no longer fathom how things went so wrong.

When my grief is a tsunami
and tears offer no release.

When survival becomes a way of life.
A life marked by unending stress and strife.

Then I have two choices.
Or rather I can wear my grief in two voices.

The voice of silence like a still lake
or the voice of fury like a roiling volcano.

It doesn't matter which choice I make.

For not every answer is wrong or right.
Not every sorrow black or white.
Shades of grey do exist.
You can't slot grief in neat array.

The Undoing

If grief were a tangible thing,
would she don it, a grey cloak?
And step into the faceless wings
among the pandemic-stricken folk.

Would she find her smile hidden
under murky street walk crags?

Would she find her sparkling eyes
where birds and beasts hide?

Would she reclaim her sweet song
from broken, half-formed shells?

Would she find her old confidence
in the breeze that called her home?

Or were these lost to her forever
leaving a hollow, empty being,
vainly scouring for what's taken
Her self-worth, identity.

Stripped off her,
peeled off her,
torn off her,
layer by painful layer
by a host of cruel slayers
with their bitter cruel words.

Battling Grief

And when the cold chill
of loneliness stalks you,
go out into the forest
and breathe in the beauty of the world.

There is an orderliness in nature
that appeals to our souls.
And when dark moments envelop you,
listen to the sweet call of the myna
at dawn trilling through the trees,
echoing through the leaves.

See how the sparrow seeks shelter
under the cupped hood of the morning glory
during a brief summer shower.
And how the sun unfailingly shows up
when clouds run dry of moisture.

And if grief still envelops you
make her your companion
and walk with her in the fields
and show her the beauty of the allamandas,
little sun cups on earth.
And the hydrangea bursting forth with beauty
like a million stars in the soil.

And if grief will not cease to be your companion,
remember, Sweet One!
Even if your life amounts to nothing more
than the nail that holds the fence together,
you are still useful and a vital part of the universe.

The Rising

The Phoenix

They march out in the darkness of the night.
The wild wind warns of their unforgiving might.

Holding torches aloft to light their path.
On either side the bog, using sticks to cut a wide swathe.

The self-righteous mob, stubborn souls rooted in false authenticity.
Seeking to vent their inner frustration on the altar of duplicity.

The wind assaults their faces, billowing at their misdirected fury.
Their eyes water with the sting; listen to the wind; be wary.

Nature defends its own; a great gust blows out torches like trifling candles.
Groping in darkness, seeking light from skies star-spangled.

Like feral beasts, undaunted, they forge on in search of their prey.
Convinced, they'll find it cowering in a state of decay.

Hadn't they already torn it to shreds; their pens unforgiving in a screaming rush?

Now all they need to do is finish the job; find their prey in the bush.

Adrenaline coursing through them; it's them against the dark.
A sweet song halts them in their tracks; is it a starling or a lark?

Laughing scornfully, they forge ahead; they have found their prey assuredly.
Hadn't they heard the song? They had quelled the voice but she sang apparently.

Heads bent low they push against the solid mass of darkness.
Stopping in their tracks, they stumble upon a pile of grey ashes.

Gripped by a strange fear they step back; glowing embers rise from the ashes.
Eyes like flame, great wings fanning the fire; the phoenix rises with a resounding crash.

And the rest is history....

My Little Blue Candle

I lit a blue candle in a shadowy room.
Shades drawn tight
against the intruder, daylight.
I watched its flickering light cast out gloom.

My little blue candle bravely shone on,
slowly melting into pools of silver-blue wax.
A mere speck in a large room, my candle still had its own act.
Against the larger dark, it clung to its shimmering own.

Is a little wick a match for a larger dark?
Can a single silent voice drown out voices raised en masse?
Carved out of truth and courage, my candle's got class.
And if you believe in magic, even candles defeat the mighty dark!

The Oppressed

Wild child! Wear your anger and anxiety like a cloak,
even as your eyes burn like hot embers.

I want to remind you that
you are valid
and so is your anger.

You never asked to live in a house of flames
while people who profess they care
pretend there is no fire.

Your distress is a valid response to the oppression you face.

Working Through Anger

Anger if allowed to fester
can become a powerful harbinger
of hate and all that is destructive.
Can anger be turned into a force constructive?

Stay with your anger; acknowledge it.
Don't strangle it, suffocate it.
Approach it gently, express it.
Allow it to course through you, breathe it.

When anger weighs into heavy,
it turns into fires unhealthy.
Step away from it, find your core.
Turn your face to the sun, cleanse, become whole.

Anger fosters creativity.
The burning embers form powerful alchemy.
Paint, write, turn embers into glittering gold
till the flames burn out, turn stone cold.

Balance your anger with everyday routines.
Slipping out of flames, hold on to moments of happy
till anger slowly loses its intensity
and you and your anger part ways finally.

Conquering Emotions

As the music slowly drifts in the mellow breeze,
she rises with the notes, moves almost absently.
Raising her hands, she sways with the beats.
Twirling to match the slow rhythm, the rising heat.

And with each pirouette she exhales it all,
the anger, the rage, the cruel taunts!
Whirling, whirling, skirts flaring,
till she is one with the beat, the rhythm, the chanting

Her hands rise to meet the blue heavens above.
Her soles sink in the soft soil of the mango grove.
As she rises to a crescendo, rising, rising,
and the Earth reaches out to her, grounding, grounding.

Her soul rises to meet the musical bars
and empties it of all the lacerations, the scars.
She is a whirling dervish, emptying the pain,
till her soul she regains; her soul she regains.

And peace and forgiveness finally reign!

From Flames to Embers

As she turns her face
to the pale blue skies,
she feels the first sting
of winter on her skin.

She drinks in the cool air,
slow,
easy,
in small gulps.

And all of the rage,
all of the fire,
bubbling like lava,
scorching,
choking,
slowly dies out.

Flames flicker into embers
and coolness quells the rage.
The dissonance between
the outer world and the inner self
slowly dissipates at the melting point of the horizon.

And she reaches out her hand hesitatingly
to grasp the tenuous threads of life
for better days.

The Strengthening

Courage

You are molded from stardust
and courage runs through your bones.

Courage that makes you show up
for the world even when
it has treated you so bad.

And you not only show up,
you show up dressed in kindness.

Courage runs through your bones
and I marvel at the thousand reasons
you find to keep going and never stop in spite of it all.

And courage courses through the very marrow
of your bones for you always believe in yourself
and choose to move forward even when
life gives you a thousand reasons to retreat.

Yes, there is fire in your eyes
and courage in your bones.
I can see it, Sweet One.

Mountains of Today, Stories of Tomorrow

And the mountains you climb today,
the insurmountable ones,
will form the stories you sing tomorrow
to your children and their children.

And that is how legends are born
and handed down over the generations.

Cheering Her On

And you owe it to the little girl inside you
who believed in magic
even when demons tore at

the very fabric of her dreams
and she was poised on the edge of the precipice
more often than she could count.

Over and over, she rode the wild beast of darkness
and chose life again and again.
And on days when you succeed

give the little girl inside
a hug and say,
"This one is for you."

Soft and Strong

And the hard iron they carry in their hearts,
I will not carry.

I will wish them well
and hope time's marching hands
will soften the hard iron in their hearts.

I will give them my courtesy
but never my complicity.

And I take back from them
that which I had given away so thoughtlessly.
Full responsibility for my life!

Strength

Even when you fall apart
and your knees hit the floor
and your grief is a tsunami
that carries you on wave after relentless wave.

You, my darling, are strong.
So very strong.

And even when you carry
silent storms in your eyes
but manage to hold yourself together
and don't relent in the face of grief.

You, my darling, are still so very strong.

And isn't that the beauty of strength?
It is a shimmering cloak and we all wear it differently.

On some, it is a silent sorrow storm
and on others, it is a hurricane.

Hidden Strength

Even when it pours inside you,
a storm churning away
and you are drowning in the deluge.

You are so beautifully strong.

You don't allow anyone to see the storm.
All they see is the sunshine in your eyes
and the laugh lines around your mouth.

And that is what makes you
so incredibly beautiful and eternally strong.

A Tale of a Rose

In a shady, woody arbor,
like a ship drawn to a safe harbor,
the waif rose seeks shelter
turning inward to her epicenter.

Ah rose! What a conundrum lies in your beauty.
Your soft dewy petals crushed so easily.
Your thorns well-hidden in your fleshy stem
speak of hidden strength, your true gems.

You fight a good fight, my rose.
You battle, vanquish, weather the blows.
You may be bowed, but never broken.
Crushed, giving off sweet fragrance, love's true token.

Your beauty's in your strength, your strength in your beauty.
When the good fight is won, you retreat in your authenticity.
You'll live to tell other tales, my rose.
For now, sleep, and spin tales of pure gold!

Wildflowers and Weeds

And I will always have great respect
for wildflowers and weeds! Look at
them growing in such gay abandon!
They don't dress themselves
with soft petals and precious buds.

Oh! Look at them dancing in all
their unadorned glory in the
summer breeze. While ruby roses

and snowy lilies yearn for water,
rich food and tender care,
wildflowers delight in their
complete unruly love for life
that defies the rules for orderly existence.

And so what if rude hands tear them
out of the soil and toss them away
to make room for prized roses?

Still they spring back to life
pushing towards the sun
through small cracks in paved stones.

Yes! I have great respect for wildflowers and weeds!

A Tale of a Tree

You are a seedling in tiny, cupped hands
planted deep in your little garden-land.
You soak water of life from rich moist soil.
Gentle hands lavish you with care and toil.

You are a little sapling, newly sprouted from moist Earth.
Your tender leaves dance to celebrate your birth.
You are a tree; you are worthy and strong
till you were caught in a great storm.

The storm blew for many a day and night.
It set your leaves in the wind alight.
The storm stole your branches, snapped your boughs.
Your tree friends trembled; many fell to the ground.

You shook in the grip of the storm's fury.
You were tired of nature's great cruelty.
Suddenly, a hush descended, had the storm stopped?
Wearily, raising your stripped bark, "is she done," you asked.

"I am the eye of the storm," she shrieked.
"How are you still standing, tell me your secret!"
"Ah! You can strip me off leaves, my branches too.
All this and more you can do!"

"But my strength lies in my roots growing deep in Mother Earth.
I have been nurturing them since I was a seedling in Earth.
And today I know just what I can withstand.
So bring on your fury; you know not my roots, my land!"

You are Enough!

And when you look around
and see others
so clever,
so much younger,
perhaps prettier,
and smarter,
bearing the burden of
grief so well.
So much stronger.

Remember this one thing!
You are enough!

And when you look around
and see others
who hold it together
with graceful ease,
so able to weather every storm,
so much better than all your sisters.

Remember this!
You are enough!

And remember this! Remember it well!
Most of your sisters are winging it,
making it up as they go along, faking it.
They are struggling but hiding it
behind smiles and faces lit
with laughter and perfection.

So you are enough!
So very enough!

On good days,
bad days,
rainy days,
sunny days,
you are so enough!

So you can choose to be different.
Embrace your enoughness
and wear it with pride
like a beautiful gown.
And when you do that
you will feel no need for
the hiding,
and the faking,
and the perfecting.
For you will have mastered the art of imperfect perfection.

The Power of Silence

And when the world goes a little crazy.
Attacks pour in from every corner.

The wisest people choose silence as an answer!
Few understand the power of silence!
It is more potent than a thousand words!

But to remain silent in the face of fury,
here is the magic formula.

You have to love yourself
fiercely, wholly, completely.
Love yourself enough to know your worth!

Self-Worth

Who decides how much you are worth?
Is it measured by the length of your hair, the size of your girth?

Who places a value on who you are?
Do they check your bank balance; do your profits and losses add?

Is self-worth a tangible thing?
The labels on your clothes; the cars you drive in?

Who decides the depth of your worth?
Is it directly proportionate to the size of your house?

Tossing aside these 'unworthy' notions,
You set out to carve a new definition.

Self-worth is being true to your inner self.
With social norms refusing to mold yourself.

And self-worth is the voice of authenticity.
It's the voice of compassion; its simplicity.

A hundred naysayers may come along,
cast aspersions on your worth; say you don't belong.

But if self-worth is limitless with roots true and deep.
Your inner strength is yours to keep.

The Healing

Duality

If breaking and shattering feel like a tsunami
then healing flows in gentle waves.
And if on some days
it feels like you are drowning in suffering,
there are other days
you ride the waves of blessed healing.

Clear Skies, Starry Nights, No Hope in Sight

Draw the shades on clear skies, starry nights.
Will the pink-hued dawn set the world right?
If dark clouds cast shadows of uncertainty,
a sliver of light reveals today's infinite possibilities.

Can you paint beauty from brush-strokes of pain?
Draw the hood of hope over your care-worn face.
And even if there is no hope left in sight,
there's always another dawn, another starry night.

Wreaths of mist envelop hills cold and blue.
Nestled in divine peace, your song runs true.
But Sweet One! Why, oh why didn't they ever tell you?
This world was never meant for one as beautiful as you.

After the Storm

No one duels with damage
and comes out unmarked.

You were so strong, Sweet One.
You didn't ask for their pity or sympathy.

But you did want a loving gesture,
a kind word, some compassion.

You didn't get it, did you?

You fought a war, Sweet One,
and you fought it alone.

Now rest, rejuvenate.
It's time to heal.

The Whispering Scars

And one day, darling,
I promise you will heal.

And your wounds will close
and the hurt will end.

But you will always carry the scars
that will remind you
of the damage that was done.

Scars that will whisper
the things that were said,
the people who turned their backs on you.

And your scars will be the badges
of the war you have fought
to become the person you are today.

Wear your scars with pride.

Three Magic Words

And looking back, do you see your life
littered with chaos
seeping out of the dark pores
of your existence?

The hurt may seem unending right now.
Release the hurt, Sweet One.

Whisper these three magic words to yourself,
"Let it go!"

And then ask yourself
what lessons did you learn from this?

Leaving the Shadows

Healing is not linear or circular. It is entering a maze without a route map. You will take many wrong turns and detours. And the goal is not to find your way out of the maze. It is to enter the very center of the maze.

True healing is an inside job. You can't heal by skirting the periphery of the maze, where your shallow feelings and emotions lie. You need to go within and connect with your inner core. There you will meet your deepest emotions and feelings. Honor them for they hold a mirror to your true self. They will show you who you were before the breaking and the person who has emerged from it.

You may never find closure. But you will seek release. And you will seek it in the people and the things that leave a warm, lingering glow in your heart. You need to unlearn the art of living and doing and relearn the art of thriving in the present moment.

Unboxing the Darkness

When life hands you boxes of darkness
all wrapped in sheaths of ugliness,
you hold your head high
draw strength from the blue of the sky.

You inhale the peace of the blue within you
and exhale the grey wreaths of ugliness from you.
And you find the strength to unbox the darkness,
the names, the cruel taunts, the bile of bitterness.

And you release it all in the wild wind.
Watch the unboxed darkness float into nothing.
And you settle in the soft grass, at last at ease.
Even wildflowers bloom in ashes of animosity.

Funeral of Sorrows

Today she chose to light a fire. She used fairy dust and pixie sparkle to keep the flames high. And in it she cast every scar, every sorrow, every shade, every shadow. The dark moments, the broken dreams and empty promises that had seared her like a shooting star, today she chose to burn them all.

And when the orange flames settled into glowing embers, she scooped up a handful of grey ash and bending over the flowing stream, she slowly opened her fist releasing the grey ash into the rippling water. And she saw in the sparkling water a lady pure and beautiful cleansed of yesterday's ugliness. And her eyes reflected hope for healthy tomorrows.

Loving the World

And when people spurn her,
she turns to nature and loves the world around her.
The clouds like soft, feathery pillows in the pale blue above.
The song of the nightingale thrills with its sweetness,
as do the soft petals of the rose against her cheek.

And so what if her footwear is worn and feet sore,
and her clothes a little worse for wear?
She hardly focuses on these trivial externals.
Her mind is so consumed by words that dance
in her head and find their way magically on her little screen.

And when she is weary of long hours of work; yet satisfied.
She can slip on her worn footwear and stroll
where peacocks dance in gay abandon,
and songbirds sing their evening song of mirth,
and the red bleeds into the grey of the horizon.

Healing

After spending days in a fog of grey murky clouds,
sunshine filtered in a burst, speaking its truth aloud.
She opened the windows shut tight against the outside world.
And let in the light and the air and bird song filled with mirth.

After days spent hidden under her duvet grieving,
it took her a long time to perceive the truth under the hurting.
Only the broken, creatures filled with pain can smash others apart.
Their lives devoid of kindness; no love in their hearts.

But only the strong can withstand such a breaking.
Taking it in their silent stride, the whiplashing, the aching.
The broken set out to steal souls.
The strong heal; make themselves whole.

The broken love breaking; smashing lives to smithereens.
An echo of the pain that fills their empty beings.
The strong are the survivors.
Reclaiming their lives; eternal fighters.

And in reclaiming, they set strong boundaries
against the broken and their unbridled fury.
This is their life; this is their home.
The broken are welcome no more; this is a no entry zone.

The Reclaiming

After a great breaking comes a great healing
and you heal in everyday things.
When you clear the cluttered surfaces,
put things away in their rightful places.

Spend long moments in the shower
allowing water to wash away yesterday's ugliness.
And step out shining and whole
ready to take on the world.

You trade in yoga pants for long-forgotten finery.
Scoop your hair behind ears; put on those beauties.
Scrub scented body butter on tired skin.
Rub shimmer in limp hair.

And light your candles,
letting music waft over you
as you reach for well-thumbed books.
Go for walks holding your face to monsoon showers.

Gaze at the blue-green beauty of a peacock.
Contemplate sun-dappled shadows playing hide and seek.
And as the soothing balm of hope envelopes your soul,
you know that soon you will step out and find your place
in the sun.

Lifting the Veil of Depression

She is a warrior queen.
She has skirted the 'eye' of grief and despair
and walked barefoot on parched Earth, beyond repair.
In her grief, she reigns supreme.

Still, she bears the scars.
Bent but not broken by sorrow.
Her laughter lost in a hidden tomorrow.
You don't duel with grief and leave unmarked.

Then while walking on parched Earth, she met Solomon.
Wiser words never were spoken.
"Heavy loads are not meant to be carried; drop your burden."
So, she practiced putting down her grief; one brick at a time.

And she noticed dew drops shining on rose petals.
Her laughter rang loud and clear, not often, but now and then.
She stopped to drink in the beauty of the world; she stopped more often.
Like sea breeze, grief lifted; soothing showers of happiness settled.

Priceless Attire

She walked in
wearing her cloak of confidence
with such grace
and effortless ease.

And all the people seated in that room
admired the peace radiating from her face.
And they whispered among themselves
what a priceless gift that peace was.

But they didn't know did they,
how long she had saved
to wear that cloak of confidence?

And the pearls of peace she wore so effortlessly
had cost her many hours of solitude
spent in quiet prayer and reflection.

And the smile that lit her face
and reflected a thousand stars in her eyes,
she had learned to draw it
from the silver linings on dark clouds
and wear it on her face and mirror it in her soul.
But that knowledge was hers to keep.

For she had learned
the hard way
that nothing in life comes easy,
not confidence,
not peace,
and not happiness.

And people find a way to destroy beautiful things.

Impossibly Imperfect

At times, the world has a way of shrouding you in blankets of expectations. Has life reduced you to a whirling dervish? Have you worn yourself out? A human doing moving in rhythms and patterns to make everyone around you smile in approval.

But, Sweet One, remember this! You don't have to be flawless all the time. You don't have to set yourself up to impossibly high standards of perfection. And then watch yourself reduced to pieces as you diminish day by day into a tight ball of resentful nothingness.

Look at the birds, how freely they fly by day and return to their nests at night. They never pause in their flight and wonder if they are doing it right. And the sun blazes across the blue moving in and out of cloudy and clear skies without stopping for a moment to pause and wonder whether it is doing it right.

And the world is calling out to you, Sweet One, to shrug off all the layers of expectation, the weight of perfection and then stand there, completely vulnerable, impossibly human, completely lovable just as you are! Step up, Sweet One! And take your place in the Universe! It is offering itself up to you! You belong here!

The Art of Healing

There is nothing beautiful about healing. It is messy and ugly with many angry strains woven in between. Healing is not a journal all neatly typed up with all your dark moments. It is ripped pages and ink splattered sheets.

It is showing up for life every single day when all you want to do is crawl between the covers and sleep. It is leaning on people especially at those times when you want to be alone with your thoughts. It is breathing and with each breath bringing the fragments of your body, heart and soul together for they have drifted far apart. It is bringing all the fragments of your soul under one umbrella where they dance in tandem to one another.

It is remembering you are a human being not a human doing. Your thoughts and feelings will create an ache that will run through to your very bones. But the ache is never constant. And when it stops you will know you can survive anything.

Healing with Love

There is always room for love.

Even when grief washes over you
in wave after relentless wave.

When the shores of survival seem
distant and unreachable.

When the tsunami of trauma
shakes you dry of every emotion.

At the end, there is always room for love.

Love acts as the most powerful ingredient
in the healing journey.

The Circle of Healing

On days when you feel like
all you are doing is regressing,
circling the same shattered
feelings again and again,
don't be hard on yourself, Sweet One.

You have come far
and your journey is not an illusion.
Healing never follows a linear path.

When you finally choose to love yourself
the pieces will fall into place.
You will heal and your feelings will heal.

Comfort in Little Things

And on days when my trauma
overwhelms me,
I take comfort in the little things.

In the rose briar that twines
and tumbles over the walls.
In the gentle sound of rain casting
freshness on earth as it falls.

In the delight of the sparrow
as it pecks the bread I have
laid out and then takes flight.

In the gentle breeze whispering
through the trees lulling me to sleep.

I remember the people who
love me unconditionally
and will never leave me.

And I hold my memories close to me
as I rock the waves of trauma
to the shores of peace.

Healing in Your Hands

We have to heal from whatever broke us.
We have to pour water over our wounds.

And allow the wind to whisper
its soothing magic over our scars.

Bathe in the silver
light of the moon.

And allow the sun-kissed flowers
to softly caress our faces.

We can't just sit there
and stare at our wounds.

We have to put ourselves first
and heal ourselves
and remind ourselves
no one is going to save us.

It is up to us to save us.

Your Healing Journey

And during your healing journey you must learn how to bathe in the waters of self-compassion. You must wrap yourself in layers of kindness. And when joy settles over your being, soothing as the first rays of sunshine, you will learn to shed the layers of pain and hurt you clung to so tightly because they had become your comfort zone. And finally, when you shed your pain, an old unwanted skin, you will rise shining and whole in the sunshine again.

An Ocean of Healing

And when you dive deep into the ocean of healing, you will first encounter the darkness of your wounds. You must swim in the darkness for a while even though it threatens to tear you apart with its shark teeth.

As you swim deeper, you will emerge from the darkness into the waters of rage. You must swim in the bloodied, red murky pools for a while but stay afloat. Do not sink into the red.

When you finally leave the waters of rage behind, you will find the cool, sea-green waters of healing soothing you in soft gentleness. And as you swim further, the darkness and the sea of red will recede into the dim recesses of your memory and you will finally emerge from the ocean a different person.

Transformation

And she made the mistake of thinking the endpoint of healing and transformation was learning to love herself. And when the world shattered her, she healed herself back into wholeness by learning to love herself. Self-love was part of her healing journey.

But the endpoint of transformation was not loving herself. It was complete surrender to the universe. When she learned to understand the journey of the clouds sliding across cerulean skies. And when the song of the birds rang sweet and true and she knew in her heart that they were singing a sweet song of hope. And when she learned to hear the secrets of the river; secrets it had gathered in its long journey before it spilled into the sea – that is when she became one with the universe and all living things. And she had not only healed but become a different person. She had transformed into a universal being.

The Ruminating

Ruminations

I have no more use for old pain.
For dark rooms without lights,
for nightmares following painful stories,
I have no more use for any of these.

For now, I focus on the gentle in every day.
My heart is sown together with
warm golden globes
that house some precious memories.

Do trees forget how to shed their leaves in October?
And what of the moon?
Does it ever forget how to wax and wane every fortnight?

Just as the recipe for these sacred events are sewn in their soul houses,
there are certain moments that will stay with me forever
reminding me of a life well-lived.

Precious Things

I used to save precious things.
Boxes and cupboards and drawers
were neatly stacked with my precious things.
That chipped China mug, a gift
from she who sparkled with laughter.
And those smooth cowrie shells
collected during a long-forgotten trip to the beach.
And the serene, smiling face of the Buddha,
his smooth visage emanating the peace I craved in life.

Till one hot summer morning,
I saw the precious things for what they really were.
Clutter!

They had slowly, almost insidiously
crept out of the drawers and cupboards
and occupied every veritable surface of my house.
And I swept up all the precious things
and gave them away.
I feel so much lighter now.
For I made the mistake of thinking
precious things house precious memories
when really it is the heart
that is a storehouse for precious things.

Nothing Lasts

I visited the House of the Dead the other day.
My eyes ran over the row of names.
Once laughing, talking, making plans for life.
Now reduced to cold stones strewn with flowers
from those who remember them with initial tears
and later fond smiles.

And I realize nothing lasts in the world.
For even memories fade with the hands of time.

Hues of Life

The rising ball of flame at dawn
Pink orange hues; nature's fount
Pink, to draw love's flavor
Orange, joy of life savor

The golden ball at its radiant noon peak
The throbbing vein of life bespeaks
A clarion call for spontaneous activity
Blooming buds herald nature's bounty

The torch of muted flame at twilight
The Blue Hour betwixt day and night
Calls to mind peace and serenity
Worldly tasks make way for creativity

When darkness descends o'er sable skies
With glittering diamonds like little eyes
The creamy orb in accord with aqua rhythms
Waxing, waning, sparks spiritualism

Twilight Panorama

Mystical skies at twilight
come along with lessons galore.

Shades of grey as day departs
blend good and bad in every heart.

Delicate orange hues remind
simple acts of being kind.

And stretching across this lyrical beauty
azure loveliness speaks of peace and purity.

Beauty in Little Things

And learn to find beauty in little things!

A little garden patch,
the smile of a new born infant,
a line out of a poem,
clouds floating dreamily in cerulean skies.

They nurture the soul.

Introspection

And she made the mistake of thinking
some days she was the river,
and some days she was a lake,
and on hard days she thought
she was just a tiny drop.

But little did she know she was
none of these things. Or maybe
she was all of these and more for she
housed an entire ocean in her soul.

All she needed to do was
break the glass barrier
of her thinking and dive deep
into the depths of her being
to discover herself.

Crafting Kind People

People are not born kind. They are made kind when life forces them to walk through the flames of trauma. The kindest souls have experienced much at the hands of life and they have turned their hard experiences into lessons of softness and compassion. Again and again, kind souls turn their faces to the warmth of the sun and choose to believe in love. Kind people are crafted at the bitter hands of fate and destiny.

Destiny and Free Will

In the tryst between destiny and free will,
how does the little human prevail?
Is life predestined...foretold in the stars?

Indeed, it is so...

Till freewill raises its leonine head
to reveal the final secret.
Be in the world but not of the world.

Happiness in Hard Times

And those who have suffered great loss
often find happiness
in the most unexpected places.

And they hug their happiness
and hold it close
guarding it fiercely like a treasured jewel.

The Art of Giving

Did you know bees sip nectar from flowers?
Yes, of course you knew this, you'll say.
But did you know flowers at dawn
unfold their shiny, dew-soaked petals
and softly whisper to the wind?
And the wind carries their word to the bees,
"Come sup on me."

The Sweetest Love

Look at the Sun freely giving off its light to the world and its warmth too, in which both flowers and bees frolic.

And look at the rain curtain gently falling to earth. Oh, how it awakens the buds to bloom. And the blooms, in turn, give freely off their nectar to the bees.

And yet never have I heard nature whisper, "you owe me." Have you seen such a sweet love in any of the books? A love that fills you with pleasure.

Look at how Apollo reaches out and warms you even as you stand before Him empty-handed, barefoot, devoid of all offerings. Do you also feel this love? Or have you joined the infernal race for money, power, possessions?

Reveling

Monsoon slid in early this year banishing blistering summer heat in a single brushstroke of rain. And just like that the dark rooms to trap cool air were a thing of the past.

I slipped outdoors again. Taking a deep breath to soak in the sweet fragrance of the rain-moistened earth. I reveled in the fat, cool drops falling on my face rolling off my cheeks.

And I wore the cool monsoon winds like a light cloak. I knew I didn't have to worry about another hot, dark summer for some time to come. And I opened my arms to the world to take my place in the nature of things.

Feisty

I light a candle in a dark room. Head bowed over pristine sheets, as I struggle to capture my muse and ink it on paper. The candle burns low. I glance at it. Will it hold till I finish my scribbling, my vain grasping after my muse?

A moth flies into the room unbidden. It hovers low over the flame. The heat singes its wings as it flies away. I watch it fluttering in the air with its blackened, flame-torn wings.

But the moth's feisty spirit remains untouched. I don't notice a hint of self-pity. Isn't that a marvelous thing?

Nurture the Soul

Things that are soul crushing:
Lies
Secrets
Manipulation
Exhaustion

Things that revive the soul from the dead:
True connections
Honest communication
Grace under pressure
Unconditional love

Earth as Poetry

And some of us don't aspire to greatness. We are content to write under the skies and smile with the flowers and nurture our little garden patch.

Some of us are content to nourish.

Eternal mothers! We forge new pathways through our art.

Special People

I know there are people who smile at plants and flowers, who delight in the flight of sparrows.

People who love the roar of the sea and the quiet of the misty mountains.

People who build houses of peace in their souls.

I know there are people like that, special people. I can understand them.

The Three Mistakes of Life

The first is loving others more than yourself.

The second is caring too much, too deeply,
be it love or friendship.

The third is living for others not for yourself.

And when the rug is pulled
from beneath your feet
and you realize years of love, years of care
have been in vain!

Your daughter looks at you
with a winsome smile.
Her simple answer rings true,
"Do you, be you, love you!"

Love is a Curious Thing!

On wet afternoons, as fat raindrops lash against her window pane, she randomly takes out the various loves hidden in her heart.

This one, so soft and beautiful, like the rosebud cheeks of a new-born!

This one, strong and enduring, meant to last a lifetime and beyond! Isn't that what the 'vows' promise?

And this one, a silly, giggly love as they shelter under the large leaf and talk about the meanderings of life!

The last of the raindrops roll down the pane, as she tucks the various loves back into her heart, content with a life well-spent.

She notices a beautiful rainbow arching across the sky in a kaleidoscope of colors reminiscent of the various hues in her life. And a little song-bird hops up to her pane to remind her of the one love she has neglected.

"It is the greatest love of all," the bird chirps before disappearing into the blue beyond and she is left wondering where to seek this love....

Conversations with the Soul

I saw her standing there by the seashore. She flung out her arms to the aqua seas. And watching her, I knew she wanted to embrace the whole universe in her little being.

I walked towards her hesitatingly. And turning, she gazed at me with soft eyes. I saw a world of love mirrored in her hazel eyes.

"Sweet One," I whispered, "before you pour yourself into the universe, learn to just love yourself."

"I don't know how," she whispered back.

And taking her hand, I guided her to the edge of the aqua waves. "Look within, Sweet One," I whispered. "You house all the answers in your little being." Smiling, I caressed her cheek softly before walking away!

"Wait!" she called out softly. "You look just like me, yet strangely different. There is an otherworldliness about you. Who are you?"

"Don't you recognize me, Sweet One? I am the Voice of your Soul."

Love's Vast Nature

She rises with the dawn and walks down to the sandy shore where white wings sweep low over the blue shallow. Her fingers claw the soft, loose sand and she rakes the softness raw till it exposes the pretty pink shells hidden in its depths.

She gathers the shells in a blue jar and plucking a cotton white cloud from the sky, she seals the salty pink in the pristine blue.

Plunging her hands into her pockets, she removes a crust of bread and breaking it neatly into half, she absently chews on one part while offering the other to the white wings.

For don't we all belong to one large family? But we must remember to love ourselves first.

An Enduring Love

And she made the mistake of thinking because she was so loved by the world, she didn't need to love herself. It was enough if she gave of herself to all in exchange for all the love they showered on her.

And then in one stroke, the world turned its back on her and love turned into the grey ashes of emptiness. And she realized the people who said they loved her were straw dolls with hollow eyes in plague-ridden fields.

She finally learned to look inward and find the most enduring love of all. She learned to love herself.

Loving Yourself

She went for a walk in the woods and crouching under the crimson bloom, she found her Rage quivering amidst the thorns. Her fingers bled as she plucked out her Rage from among the thorns.

Red drops glistened against the snow-driven path and she watched the red heat melting into the cold white till it consumed her no more.

The dim glow from the window beckoned her back. And sheltering in its warmth, she felt a curious emptiness within that had housed the Rage for so long.

And at last…. She found room in her heart to love once more. She reflected on the love she had given so freely, scattering it carelessly like confetti on friends and family. And standing there in the warm cocoon, wrapping her arms around herself, she finally learned to give that love to herself.

The Heart of Self Love

You were never made to fit into neatly woven molds.
You were made to be YOU!
And when you learn to love yourself enough,
you will accept all the bits of you that go into making you.

The small bits, the large bits, the pretty bits, the ugly bits,
they all go towards defining you.

And this forms the basis of self-love.
It is self-acceptance;
learning to accept all the bits you house within you.

And learning to love yourself just as you are,
the messy you,
the perfectly imperfect you,
the kind you,
the silent you,
the soft you.
Just You!

From Flawless to Flawsome

I walked away one day from the old picture-perfect version of me. The flawless version with hunched shoulders, my spine impossibly arched as I bent backwards to please others and wore their approval and opinions like perfect pearls around my shrinking neck.

I walked away and found waiting a woman tall and beautiful who wore love with such effortless ease like a beautiful garment stitched with gossamer threads of compassion and wisdom. And draped around her slender shoulders was a cloak of abundant kindness that lent such grace to her stature.

She held out her arms invitingly. And I walked up to her melding into her. She had been waiting for me for a long time, she whispered, for she was my new self, the grown self, the transformed self.

I stepped forth hesitatingly wearing my garment of love with confident ease for it belonged to me. The hollow spaces in my soul that I had desperately filled with my craving for love from others was now filled to the brim and overflowing with this great powerful love that throbbed within me.

A love no one could ever take away from me.

A love that would never betray or let me down.

A love that would stay with me for the rest of my life.

A love that was unconditionally mine.

And with straight back and squared shoulders, I walked to the gilded frame and she stared back at me.

My love!

She belonged to me.

She was me!

Soul Song of Self-love

When your mind is hard on you, hold each hard thought in the palm of your hand and blow it softly into the universe, till all the hard thoughts are transformed into glistening rainbow bubbles floating into the blue beyond.

Let your heart radiate the joyous pink rays when your heart sings its soul song of self-love.

Hope is the Song I Sing

Hope is the song I sing
when I watch the clouds gather over parched land.
Will the clouds hear my hope song?
And answer it with a gentle rain song?

And hope is the song I sing
when my ship is caught in a crescendo of waves.
Will the waves hear my hope song?
And answer it with a smooth wave song?

And hope is the song I sing
when September winds strip leaves from trees.
Will the wind hear my hope song?
And answer it with a green leaf song?

And yet hope remains an eternal song on my lips,
trilling in my veins, singing in my soul.
Stretching across the vastness of infinity
to embrace life's endless possibilities.

The Pink-rimmed Dawn of Hope

The flaming torch of the setting sky;
the Blue Hour betwixt day and night.
Twilight heralds cosmic dichotomy.
Your Animagus spews poison or honey.

The Mystic Hour chants sacred rites;
whispered promises of a new light.
Rousing souls from the nocturnal sea
towards the sparkling light of eternity.

As dawn breaks in the pink-rimmed sky,
hope eternal spirals high.
Buds blossom from blackened plague.
A new life, we celebrate!

Earth, it's now your turn to breathe.
Flowers blossom under verdant leaves.
Birds soar free in cerulean skies
and people remember how to smile.

Dolphins frolic in aqua seas.
Nature dances in cosmic symphony.
People shed old ways for new.
Love and kindness are given their due.

The charred soil blooms anew.
Gratitude blossoms, relationships renew.
Healing light spills like mellifluous rain.
Dawn sky heralds, "let's begin again!"

Yellow Blossoms of Joy

We walked down our shady avenue.
Yellow blossoms bursting with joy.
We ruminate on the year gone by.
The year of the pandemic; a year to review.

Our mind-head gazes over 2020.
A year of beauty and ugly in equal measure.
Home and hearth we learned to treasure.
And the virus raging within humanity changed the course of history.

And the new year carries hope in the air.
Hope that hugs will once more be free from fear
and we'll freely cherish all we hold dear.
As the yellow blossoms whisper promises of mindful care.

The Growing

Flowers of Forgiveness

Bell-shaped flower in glorious bower
rising with the morning sun,
climbing in a wondrous shower,
your beauty truly matches none.

Changing color as the day goes by,
blazing violet, hues of pink.
Finally, settling with a silent sigh
into folded petals as if to think.

Dazzling briefly, glorious flower,
I marvel at your humility.
Blooming, withering in a few hours,
your withering beauty breeds forgiving serenity.

Reminding not every life is black or white.
Not every answer wrong or right.
Every life has shades of grey.
You can't slot life in neat array.

It's Never Personal

When frown lies crease your forehead
and storm clouds brew overhead.
This simple song, darling, you sing,
It's just not a personal thing.

When arrows like bitter darts strike.
Heavy wreaths of dislike smite.
Be kind to yourself; don't take it hard.
Look at yourself; you're brave, you're smart.

What people do to you
is almost never about you.
They project on you their insecurities;
their illusions; their realities.

When you wear a strong armor,
the slings, the barbs, they cease to matter.
They'll slide off you in a fluid motion.
Water gliding off feathers into oceans.

So, enter into this firm agreement
betwixt your soul and your higher self.
No thing, no situation is ever personal.
It's just a projection of another's illusion.

Plunging Into Your Life's Purpose

She walked along the seashore on a summer afternoon. The waves rolled in, rolled back.

She stood for a long moment, shading her eyes against the brilliant sun. The sea danced in the fiery sun wearing a million diamonds on its waves.

She longed to run into the sea and scoop up the diamonds waves and rise wet from the aqua waters with a soul satisfied. For she would have met her life's purpose among the waves.

But she chose to continue walking along the shore ruminating, as she skirted the waves rushing in and avoiding the pebbles and stones on the sandy path. While the wind whispered to her, "take the plunge, take the plunge."

Don't Quit

Don't quit if your soul is in darkness entwined.
Honey, you're so close to the finish line!

Don't quit when despair gnaws at your bones.
Honey, you're so close to the finish line!

Don't quit because you feel it's too late to arrive.
Honey, you're so close to the finish line!

Honey, don't you see!
You are not too early;
you are not too late;
you are right on time
to reach the finish line.

Being Present

Trees fold their leaves at night
with a silent sigh in the moonlight.
Sleeping sweetly under star-crusted skies,
rustling leaves whisper promises of dawn light.
Unfolding at the first pink streaks in the pale sky.
Shaking dew drops off and arching towards the light.

Reminding us of the rhythm of life
with its endless wrongs and rights.
The gentle night always enfolds
the promise of a new dawn
like the sparkle of fresh green grass
on endless lawns.

Yesterday lies buried
in the recesses of the past.
Let it go, let it go, to the present moment hold fast.

Live in the Moment

Hey you! With the stars in your eyes and the rosebuds on your cheeks. Erase those creases from your brow. They don't belong there.

Cease standing in the shadows, Sweet One, bemoaning the darkness in your life. Instead let the cold past remain in the dark recesses of yesterday. Today is your day! Own it! Step up fully and take your place in the sun.

Live Like a Butterfly

These gay color-winged beauties
radiating freedom in flower fields.
Yet here's a secret borne by these happy insects.
A seven-day life span; all they can expect!

What if you had to wrap your life into a seven-day span?
How would you enfold your hours into this brief wing-span?
Would you fill your life with gay abandon?
Shower love and laughter on all companions?

If seven days is all you had?
Would you nurture your passion; make your soul glad?
Would you live each day to the full like the winged beauties?
Sipping nectar from flowers; ignoring all things ugly?

Mindful Living

I sit by the riverbank,
pulling out my list of tasks.
The list has gone blank.
Casting it in the river, in the sun I bask.
The tasks can wait for another day.
My chattering mind goes still.
Like the quiet ripples in the river bay,
from my mind-river, peace does spill.

Then what I am afraid of enters my world.
The endless motion of life entraps me.
But now I spin mundane threads into pure gold
and the fear of the whirlwind leaves me.
I become one with the whirlwind; I dance in the wind.
The wind and I, together we sing
in perfect harmony with every microcosmic thing.

To Perish or Flourish

And those who choose to make their homes in the past
will surely be caught in the cold web of darkness
in which their souls will perish.

But those who glory in the beauty of the present moment
will surely move towards the golden light
in which they will flourish.

So what do you choose today for yourself, Sweet One?
To perish or flourish?

Fika Moments

The heady aroma of strong coffee,
rain on my face; the smell of moist Earth.
Curled up in solitude, my book, my poetry, just me.
Fika moments, slow down, savor life's true worth.

A Tale of Time

Sands of time, precious, flowing,
slipping through fingers, minutes melting.
Thinking life is long but time is fleeting.

Abandon the past shrouded in shadowy history,
look not to the future veiled in mystery.
Carpe Diem! The present moment's ablaze with glory.

Be like the Tree

Grow roots deep
to draw love and friendship from the soil of life.

Open your branches to the Sun
to receive the blessings of sunshine and joy on your life.

Nourish your life tree.

The Rejoicing

A Song of Gratitude

Gratitude comes in many forms.
Savoring the calm after the storm.
A simple prayer for the morning light.
The joys of home fill hearts with delight.

The thanks we offer for food and friends.
Health in hard times; little odds and ends.
For the year that has turned full circle.
For love that never dims, retaining its sparkle.

For simple moments of sheer happy.
A winter day; two mugs of tea.
For days when I can take it easy.
And for others when I have enough to keep me busy.

For hugs and cuddles that warm the heart.
For furry paws, long walks, little talks.
For people who never give up on me.
For those who stay through the rough and ease.

Softness

Softness is the most wonderful quality in the world, isn't it?
One only has to look at nature to understand this beauty
of softness.

The soft caress of the wind,
the soft petals of a flower,
the soft whisper of the gentle rain,
the softness of the first rays of sunlight.
How they delight!

And what of the soft-spoken?
Nature's children, shall we hold them close?

A Pocketful of Emotions

Love is:
Burying your face in delicate pink blossoms.
The warmth of his breath before the world wakes.
The soft glow from long wordless hugs.
His large hand clasping your small one keeping you safe.

Joy is:
Sunshine bathing your face from cloudless skies.
The echo of songbirds trilling in your heart at dawn.
The ecstasy deep within you when words flow effortlessly.
The silent rapture of a peacock dancing in blue-green melody.

Kindness is:
Flowers offering nectar to bees and butterflies.
A young hand helping a wrinkled one up the stairs.
A dish of food left out for stray dogs and alley cats.
Just doing good and not telling a soul about it.

Peace is:
The face of the creamy moon in the serene lake.
A baby gently rocking in your soft arms.
The stillness within, the bliss of solitude.
Drawing the duvet, sinking into oblivion.

Contentment:
The colors of love, joy, kindness, peace;
this beautiful rainbow in your soul blend.
When these emotions mingle and meld,
they create a continuum of contentment
till journey's end.

Joy in Everyday Things

As you step out of the clouds of pandemic grey,
look at the world with new eyes, new ways.
Cast aside the virus despair!
Settle into the space betwixt yesterday and today.

Relish the simple, the ordinary, the everyday.
Lie in bed; soft whisper of wind, what does it say?
The green of the trees call out to you.
You draw in their energy like magic dew.

Nestled in the cocoon of the familiar;
warm blanket against the first chill of winter.
Steam from thick broth rises to your face.
His hands comfort, fingers interlace.

Joy in September

I rose with the bird call on a September Sunday,
and came upon a secret silver stream on my pathway.
Was the pandemic real; was it just a bad dream?
Seeking answers, I glanced into my silver stream.

The grey storm clouds slowly drifted away.
And the sun smiled down warming the day.
My silver stream shimmered with golden light.
And my heart soared with sheer delight.

Dipping my fingers in the silver-gold waters,
I wrapped a sliver of light around my fingers.
Silver-gold sliver wedded to me,
my heart soared in ecstasy.

The East wind whispered in the great oak trees
of joy and happiness and all creatures free.
Smiling, I raised my hands and drew the wind to me.
Wrapping it around my being like an invisible sheath.

My heart was full with the song of the wind.
And the silver-gold light wedded to my being.
My song of joy blew away the grey clouds.
The silver-gold light melded with my soul song.

Silver-gold song burst into flowers and leaves.
Birds soared in gay symphony.
Flowers danced in ecstasy.
And joy traversed from leaf to leaf.

Blending Life's Colors

My family is my Pink crayon, the one I use to color love into my life.
My friends are my Rainbow crayons, the ones I use to color laughter into my life.
Nature's lyrical beauty is my Blue crayon, the one I use to color peace into my life.
God is my Purple crayon, the one I use to blend spirituality into my life.

The Blooming

The Blooming

You bloomed through the shattered glass and the broken shards. You still managed to bloom.

When people wrote you off as broken and beyond redemption, you rose and you bloomed.

Yes! You still managed to bloom!

You broke again and again like a wave dashing against rocks and then in a beautiful water arc with rainbow mist, you bloomed.

You became the woman you are today because you rose from the depths and you bloomed. You rebuilt yourself from the shards of brokenness. And through all the breaking, you managed to retain all that is natural and free in your nature so that you could bloom exactly where you are planted.

I almost believe you broke to bloom. And no one can take this away from you.

Also a Prayer

And a morning walk where you escape into stillness and silence and watch the world slowly come to life is also a prayer.

And the time you spent in quiet reflection at your window as you watched rain wash the world clean is also a prayer.

Any time spent with HIM in your heart is a prayer.

He Exists!

I have no time for logic and reason. Let the burden of proof rest with those who need it.

I am too enthralled by the magical miracles that surround me every day. Aren't they all the proof I need?

Waking to the dawn chorus of songbirds cooing from trees heralding He has painted a fresh new day for us. And the sun that never fails to show up every morning bathing the world in its gentle, healing glory reminding us that He has given us a fresh start each morning.

And the buds that burst open into flowers. Flowers, I think, are smiles from God on Earth.

I am too enthralled by these miracles to grope in the shadowy recesses of logic and reason and ask for identity papers proclaiming His existence. For He lives in the peace that houses my soul.

Taking It in My Stride

Now when things go wrong and bad things happen, I no longer lose my temper or rail against fate. For I emptied myself of rage long back.

I realize that God has placed me exactly where I need to be at that moment to learn exactly what He needs me to learn. So now I accept the good and bad with graceful ease. Nothing disturbs my peace.

For the good brings a warm glow to my heart. And as for the bad, well, isn't experience the best teacher in the world?

Soul of a Gypsy

I have the soul of a gypsy.
I own nothing, I belong to nobody.
The green grass offers me the softest pillow.
How sweet is the breeze as it wafts over me.

I have the soul of a gypsy.
I own nothing, I belong to nobody.
The creamy orb offers me light at night.
My home is the azure arch over me.

I have the soul of a gypsy.
I own nothing, I belong to nobody.
I drink from sweet, sparkling spring waters.
The tree offers its sweet berries to me.

I have the soul of a gypsy.
I own nothing, I belong to nobody.
The sweetest rise of land houses my soul.
The wild outdoor beckons to me.

I have the soul of a gypsy.
I own nothing, I belong to nobody.

On Understanding

I used to love surrounding myself with flowers. Scattering fragrant rose petals in crystal bowls and bunches of lavenders and lilies in vases.

I especially liked placing flowers at the altar of my devotion. They never complained or spoke against me for plucking their lives so carelessly from their mother plants. Instead, they gave off their lives willingly for a few moments of my pleasure.

One morning, while I was decorating my altar with these mute offerings, it dawned on me that they liked it best when they were dancing in the summer breeze in the sunshine.

I love flowers. Now I savor their company during my morning walks. And I like to think they whisper thanks for no longer enclosing them in cement walls. They prefer to wither and fall to Mother Earth. And when I reach down to them, it is to softly caress their petals.

A Peaceful Performance

Look at the blue-green globe soundlessly moving around the golden fiery orb. Such a great journey it sets out on in peace every day. And doesn't tell a soul about it. It just goes about its business without a fuss.

And here we are, little humans so absorbed in the noise and clamor, the ups and downs of our infinitesimal lives. And if there is one thing we can learn from the blue-green globe we call home, let that one thing be the art of silent peace.

Wishes

Bury your wishes deep in your heart. Keep them like treasured secrets. Don't allow the prying eyes of the world and curious tongues to snatch your wishes from you.

When a wish remains a secret, it wraps itself with a certain magical power that lends itself to manifestation.

Just like seeds buried deep in the ground manifest into a beautiful garden. If you want to manifest your wishes, keep them secret, for the world has a habit of destroying that which it can neither see nor understand.

Inner Peace

Storm clouds blow over the seas of life. At every turn, we face stress and strife. Our little life boat is rocked to the core. We wonder, will we sink in the storm or make it to the shore.

Storm waves lap at the life boat as it rocks in the sea. Riding the high of the troughs, plunging the depths of the deep. Despair settles over us; it is a losing battle we face. We rise, we fall, we progress, we regress.

Cold fingers of fear clutch at our beings, for we know there is no way to control this tempestuous sea. So, we settle in our boats, leaving the sea to its stormy pace, while we dive into the depths of our inner space.

The wild world recedes; its calm at the core of our being. Why did we worry about the tempestuous out-of-control sea?

Closing our eyes, we settle into our inner selves, into an ocean of bliss.

Opening our eyes, we see a shooting star. Blessings flow in a golden shower.

Closing our eyes, we settle into our core. Cleansed of the ugly, shining and whole.

The wild world recedes into a calm gentle sea. And we settle into the bliss of inner peace.

Reaching for the Unreachable

I like to reach for the unreachable. My arms are wide open to receive them. Reaching for the wind that sings through the trees, and the clouds that float so effortlessly across the cerulean skies, and the gulmohar spreading its orange flames across its leafy home, and catch a fleeting glimpse of goldfish darting in the aqua waters, and the kingfisher, a little flash of blue against verdant leaves.

And as I reach out for all these unreachable things, I silently pray. I don't feel the need to bow my head in devotion for I know God is present here in every leaf and every silent whisper of the wind.

Long ago, I gave up the notion of finding him at the stony alter. I realized He didn't live in stone idols but in the living, throbbing life of nature in the blue, blue air.

Morning Musings

It is 5:00 a.m. and the palm trees are gently swaying in the monsoon breeze. The first drops of rain splatter the palms, slide off the leaves and fall into the green grass below. The roots get their fair share as do the silver threads of grass under earth.

But I barely notice this magic. So busy am I scribbling in my notebook till the incessant cooing of the songbirds, a violin strumming through the leaves, breaks my writing reverie.

I raise my head from the letters in my notebook and my breath catches in my throat as I feast my eyes on the beauty before me.

The Bliss of the Divine

You wake to silent, sable skies.
Seeking to capture the first light.
Settling into the sacred space betwixt morn and night.
As pink streaks the sky; the moon takes flight.

The silent dawn stirs with bird call.
Lashes shut as the first gold bathes your soul.
Withdrawing from without; stepping into the bliss of your inner being.
Your soul sends peace along the seven-centered rings.

God – the Weaver

Weave your life
with compassion, kindness and gratitude.
God will provide the threads.

Finding God

The pious indulge in prayers. The spiritual bask in divine ecstasy. But the truth is the palace in the sky is still far, far away. Out of reach, unreachable and most of us are still sleeping the sleep of delusion.

So What?

So what if I am an early riser waking with the dawn call of sweet song birds?

So what if I am enthralled by trees and smile in wonder when I see a bud unfurl slowly into a beautiful bloom?

And so what if I talk to jasmine flowers praising their sweet fragrance and hug oleanders for their delicate blush of pink beauty?

So what if I choose long walks in blue-green hills and solitude over noise and clamor? So what if I choose to live in the honeycomb of my mind where peace reigns supreme? So what?

So what if I scorn fame and applause and choose to step out of the race to dance to my own tune? So what?

Can anything equal the thrill that runs through me when the first primroses bloom and the quickening of my breath when I catch sight of beautiful wildflowers growing in gay abandon, as far as the eye can see?

Look at the peacock dancing to its own rhythm in all its fan-shaped blue-green majesty. At fifty, I think the peacock is a bird of breath-taking beauty. I thought so when I was fifteen as well. And so what?

So what if I pondered over what to do with my precious life and chose to walk barefoot in green grass to admire wildflowers and bees? So what, indeed! So what?

The World at its Best

Hello World! You, who are still sleeping. There is peace at dawn, which I can't find at any other time of the day.

It's almost magical this time of day. These first hours of the morning, when the sky is still dark with faint patches of light glimmering through the velvet sable. A stray bird chirps sleepily.

The world slumbers on while I sit with my head bowed either in devotion or immersed in creativity.

The large, dark pear-shaped silhouettes rustle peacefully in the morning breeze.

It's dawn and in a few hours the noise and bustle of the world will swallow the peace and light will swallow the last dark hour. But for now, I couldn't ask anything more from the world.

Reaching for Heaven

Heaven is the wind whispering in the leaves.
The soft caress of nature against my cheeks.
I raise my hands to hold fast her comfort.
Ah! To keep nature's caress with me eternally is heaven for me!

And heaven is the bird call in magical symphony.
The musical notes rising, falling in a crescendo.
In vain, I raise my hands to capture the trilling notes.
Ah! To draw out that music with ease is heaven for me!

Heaven is the butterflies dancing under a cherry blossom tree.
The amber-gold liquid spilling from soft pink petals.
In vain, I try to cup nature's ambrosia in my little hands.
Ah! To taste the amber-gold trickling down my throat is heaven for me!

Heaven is the dancing wave on golden sands.
The froth of nature's beauty, now on gold, now on aqua lands.
The wave caresses my hand for a fleeting moment before fleeing.
Ah! To hold the dancing wave in the palm of my hand is heaven for me!

Why is heaven forever out of my reach?
Why can't I keep her azure beauty eternally with me?
The wind chuckles and whispers heaven's true secret,
"Oh, foolish one! Heaven resides in your soul! You carry it within thee!"

Made in the USA
Columbia, SC
05 November 2024